Thoughts of Healing Families

The Reflections of Their Grief

Lisa Renee
Hutchins

Contents

PAINFUL DENIAL

THE ANGER WITHIN

DAY BY DAY

THE NEW PATH

AFTER THOUGHTS

Inspiration

My inspiration for this book is to share my thoughts on what it is like to experience the loss of a loved one, the various emotions we experience, and the process it takes to learn how to live without them.

Life is a precious gift we get to share with others. Many of us get to live a long life with opportunities to build a legacy, while others' time is cut short; leaving the earth before their loved ones were able to let go.

We must travel this undiscovered journey through the shock of never seeing someone we love again, trying to figure out how to deal with our feelings, accepting the loss, and moving forward with the ability to celebrate the loved ones we miss. We all go through each stage and can learn that we are not alone on our healing journey.

Dear Healing Families

I send my sincere condolences to all my readers who have lost someone dear to their hearts. We will never get over the loss, but over time, we learn how to navigate and cope with their absence. We learn to speak their name in joy instead of tears, listen to their favorite songs with a smile in our hearts instead of changing the station. We celebrate their legacy by sharing the memories that bring laughter and love to our hearts.

I hope you see yourself in this book and know that you are not alone or the only person who has had to continue this journey called life, having to leave some people behind but never to be forgotten.

Painful Denial

The Call

Answering the phone

Was routine

Never changing my life

Until the day

The person on the other end was a stranger

Delivering condolences for my loss

Sharing the news

That my loved one was gone forever

Frozen in Time

You hear the person talking
But you're unable to process the tragic news

In a fog
Overcome with devastation
Bleeding from your heart

Frozen in time
Wishing this was a dream

Realizing this reality
Is your worst nightmare

Standing frozen in time
As the world is moving around you

Too Late

The call came

Quickly he froze in time

Fear struck his face

Frantically he tells his wife and the kids they had to go

Piling the family in two cars

He takes off in a hurry

As his wife tries to keep up

He is swerving through the cars

Almost running red lights

Rushing to get to the hospital

She arrives behind him

To join all the family crying outside

Screaming in agony in each other's arms

We were too late

The Tragic Elevator Ride

She hesitantly gets on the elevator

Pushing the button to the fourth floor

To meet her new baby twin nieces

The elevator doors open

She walks into the room

Trying to face the family

Holding back tears of sadness

Knowing tragedy loomed in the emergency room downstairs

The adults all hugged with heavy hearts

She took her teenage nephew to the elevator

To bring him to the emergency room

Where the other half of the family was hysterically crying

Trying to create small talk with her nephew

Knowing his life was about to change forever

Discovering his mother, I just spoke with a few hours earlier

Tragically passed away

Tick Tock

Tick tock
Goes the hands of the clock
Each minute feels heavier than the next

Counting down the days
Until they have to visit the funeral home
To plan his celebration

They look through his closet
As the tears stream down their cheeks
They find his football jersey
Still smelling like practice with the boys

One by one, they select his outfit
Picking his Hawaiian shirt and short combination
Adding his brown Hawaiian slides and Kukui nut lei
Placing them in his light blue Nike bag
Zipping it slowly

Numb to the Touch

I am present
But lost in time

Unable to feel anything
But a shocking numbness

Being asked question after question
But having no answers

Making immediate decisions
But unable to process what is transpiring

People hug me in sorrow
But have no idea how shattered I am

Crumbling piece by piece
But wearing a mask of strength

In efforts to not completely lose it
But knowing it's just a matter of time

The Door of Reality

We park, waiting for our appointment
Trying to pull our emotions together
We laugh about the old times
In an effort to muster up a smile

The time has come,
Walking to the door
We don't want to open

In there is where you lay
Resting
Waiting for us
To plan your celebration

We pick
Your plot, casket, flowers
Arrange a date, music, and memories
Putting in place a day I never want to come

We finish your arrangements
Stopping by a room to see you for a moment
Trying to grasp what is happening

We slowly let go of your hand
Walking down a long hallway
Hearing the low, subtle music in the background
While families walk by with sorrow in their hearts

We open the door
Leaving you behind
Walking away from the door
That changed our lives forever

Living a Nightmare

Waking up without her husband
Is like living a nightmare
From the minute she opens her eyes

Rolling over to his side of the bed
Only to hold his pillow
That smells just like his spring-fresh shampoo

Dragging herself out of bed
To brush her teeth
At their dual sinks

She stands on his side
In hopes of feeling his presence
Using his towel
Looking into his side of the mirror

Staring at the shower

Stepping into its warmth

She glides down the shower wall, sitting

As the tears stream down her face

Collecting herself

To move through her day

She wakes up the kids

Smiling with a shattered heart

As it continuously bleeds through the bandages

That are barely holding it together

Driving the kids to school

Gets harder knowing that holding the house down alone

Did not result in her soldier coming home alive

Now, it was just her leading the family

Arriving at work with a smile

While everyone doesn't know what to say

She dives into her projects

As a temporary distraction, relieving her from the pain

She cooks his famous lasagna

Keeping his spirit alive

Bringing a smile to their children's faces

As they reminisce about the good times

She tucks the kids into bed

Saying Daddy's favorite prayer

Kissing them goodnight

Slowly walking down the hallway

She goes into the bedroom they shared

Washing her face alone

Crawling under their warm down blanket

Reminding herself that God has a plan for their family

Even if this nightmare is unbearable

Keep Moving

The mind moves rapidly
Jumping from one thing to the next
Making rash decision after decision

The anxiety builds
As people are constantly coming and going
Calling and texting
Inundating them with visitors, food and family

The body is afraid to slow down
Fearful of falling apart
Feeling the weight of the loss
They have to bare

Preparing An Angel

Waking up in agony
As they silently count the days
Until they have to say goodbye

The daughters gather with love in their hearts
Fixing their mother's hair and white hat
Dressing her in an elegant white suit
Gently applying her makeup
Getting her ready, as a family, one last time

The next day
They arrive early to decorate the viewing room
Filling it with her family portraits and her favorite yellow roses
Family and friends come from all around the world
To hold her hand, fellowshipping in her presence
One last time

The Anger Within

Ahhhhhh!

Sitting in their favorite spot
In the bleachers before the game
Under a warm, blue fleece blanket

He replays their football game nights
Over and over again

The coach's motivational speeches before the game
The team jumping up and down in hype mode
The band playing our fight so loud
We can feel it in our chest

You pounding on my shoulder pads
Hitting my helmet
Getting us ready to win the game

But now the locker room is silent

Without your presence

My biggest motivator

Was taken from me

Not sure how to find the motivation

Fighting for the college scholarship we both wanted

I'm so angry I have to get us there

Alone

The Raging Waters

The waves crash relentlessly
Swaying back and forth
With no rhyme or reason
Destroying everything in sight

The crests tower above the sea
Intimidating all who see
With no fear or concern
Pushing away everyone

The undertow hiding underneath it
Waiting for its next victim
With all intents and purpose
To capture and destroy whatever is within reach

One Question...Why?

Why did I miss your call?

Why was I not there?

Why didn't you tell me you needed help?

Why wasn't my love enough?

Why did you think life would be better without you?

Why did you leave us?

With My Eyes Closed

The memories slowly replay in my mind
I remember your smile
Something that warmed my heart

I hear your voice
Something that brought me comfort

I see your face
Something that filled me with joy

I feel your touch
Something that protected my soul
Memories I can only see with my eyes closed

Within the Tornado of Emotions

On the outside
The destruction of his anger is fierce
Triggered by any slight change in his environment
Blowing aimlessly with no direction

Not bothered by the hurt he causes others
As the pain inside swallows him whole
Raging at any opportunity
Forcing people to run away

When all he needs is acknowledgement
That the pain is real
Reflecting a cry for help
That is untamable to everyone
Turning him into someone he can't control

Are You OKAY?

Do I look okay?
Is the response she wants to say.

Would you be okay?
Is the question she wants to ask them.

What does okay mean?
It's just one step away from her not being ok.

What does okay look like?
It's one trigger away from her breaking down.

Unanswered Questions

Do you think about me?

Do you miss our laughter?

Do you miss my smile?

Do you anticipate hearing my voice?

Do you count the days until we meet again?

Do you think about the times we shared?

Do you have plans for our future?

Do you want a family?

Do you want to grow old without me?

Faces of Revenge

The rage builds stronger and stronger
Every day that goes by without you

How are they free to roam the earth
While you are in spirit watching down on us from above?

The need to want to inflict pain on another
Believing it will heal the devastation they caused you

How do they live with themselves
While we rage in anger at their careless behavior?

The ability to learn to breathe freely
Knowing you do not want to repeat the cycle of pain

The Claws Come Out

Death brings out the predators
The undeserving, lurking in the shadows
Silently waiting
For the right time to sneak in

To only be present for a moment
Attempting to claw their way through the family
In an effort to gain something
They feel entitled, too

They drag some meat back through the dirt
Into the darkness
Proudly holding their ungrateful heads high

Once again, staying hidden
Stalking their family silently
From a distance
Until the next family member falls

Finally Free

Today, God took you home
You are finally free
From the pain and suffering

You no longer
Have to sit in silence
Waiting for the medication
You yearn to relieve the torment of your illness

We hold your hands
Selfishly not wanting to let go
Of your spirit
Of your presence

But we know
You are finally free

Day by Day

You vs Me

You are saddened

Saying you are sorry for my loss

Sending flowers of acknowledgment

Bringing over meals from the heart

Hugging me to bring comfort

Expressing your temporary support

In hope I will be ok

I am in shock

Saying thank you, with tears rolling down my face

Seeing the beautiful flowers reminding me you're gone

Unable to eat the food made with love

Receiving hugs that can't erase the pain

Feeling an endless numbness

Unsure if I will survive

How Are You?

A question asked

Out of care

In the midst of uncertainty

Awaiting a response

Not reflecting one's true state

Just the band-aid needed to hold us all together

Creating an environment

Fragile to the touch

Breaking at the sound of our tears

In Bed, I Lie

In bed, I lie

Lifeless

Smothered by the weight of your absence

Drained from the emotional roller coaster

In bed, I lie

Invisible

Hiding from facing the world alone

Afraid I won't survive

In bed, I lie

Remembering

Your words of strength that always kept me going

Motivating me on my journey through life

In bed, I lie

Encouraged

Planning my next steps to get up and heal

Guiding me on a path to make you proud

Rise Another Day

The morning sun peaks through the window
Slowly warming his face
Waking him once again

He feels the love of her shining down
Slightly holding his blanket
Remembering her morning hugs

He sits up, absorbing the warmth of her love
Starting his day
Lighting the way

He smiles, thanking her for the love
Inspiring his heart to keep going

He stands up
Taking the steps to move forward
One day at a time

You Bleed, I Bleed

When your heart is bleeding
Mine bleeds for you

When your sadness streams down your face
My love is there to dry your eyes

When your trauma seems unbearable
My struggles allow us to laugh at the pain

When your loneliness feels cold
My hugs warm your soul

We bleed to grow
As one

Together Forever

Rolling Emotions

As I listen to your story
The pain swells inside my chest

Trying to focus on my tasks at hand
Walking you through the process
Discussing what is planned and needed

Taking your family on a park tour
Guiding you through the selection process

As we sit back at the table
Making one difficult decision after another
I look up to see you crying

The pain of the discussion we share hits home
I slowly pause, trying to regain my composure
But the emotions stream down my face

I apologize

Trying to speak without crying

As I grab tissues

Passing one to everyone

Making a light-hearted joke

The laughter is appreciated by all

As we dry our tears together

When we finished our appointment

The emotions turn to hugs of compassion

Allowing me to embrace a family

I am honored to serve

Unintentional

My reactions are unintentional
But are damaging
To the ones I love
To the ones I need

One minute, I feel happy
Ready to face the world
Enjoying my friends and family

Then, all of a sudden
I am triggered

By a smell
A joke
Or a person
Even by my surroundings

I react with sarcasm, disrespect or fear

Pushing away the ones I love

To mask the painful reminders

I'm afraid to fall

Eyes of Pain

Deep emotions pierce my heart as we speak
You smile with strength on the outside

Because you are trying to be the rock
You have always been for us all on the inside

But I can see right through them
The sadness runs deep

Keeping you so busy
Allowing you to ignore the devastation swelling inside

Consuming yourself with tasks
Staying numb to the emotions inside

In fear they will change you forever
Turning you into someone you can't free yourself from

So, you stay in denial

Resisting the desire to admit you are not ok

Even though we see the pain every day

Senseless

No value for another's life
Runs deep

Seeing the family left behind
Experiencing the loss of a community
Discovering the assassination of a role model

No consideration for another's family
The unexpected financial devastation
The hole left in the family
The children left to fill an irreplaceable void

No desire to be accountable for the trauma
To the victim's family
To the accuser's family
For the safety of the community

Masking Darkness

What Could Have Been

All the boys and girls
Play at the park

Chasing each other around the playground
Sliding down the twisty yellow slides
Swinging on the blue and black swings
Racing across the metal monkey bars

Laughing and smiling
Embracing the moment
With no care in the world
Or thought about where life may lead them

Not knowing
The joy their happiness brings
To a parent
Who lost their child too soon

She watches in hopes of healing
Her broken heart

Supporting and loving
The children that are still with her
Trying to be present in the moment
She is struggling to accept

Never Got the Chance

I never got the chance

To hear your first cry

To see your precious face

To hold you in my arms

To feel your heartbeat against mine

To smell your baby-fresh aroma

I never got the chance

To change your little diaper

To dress you in your blue outfit

To snuggle you in your blue fuzzy blanket

I never got the chance

To put you in your car seat

To ride home with you, our family of three

To see you sleeping soundly in your new crib

To run to your rescue the first time you woke up crying

I never got the chance

To say thank you for the journey we shared

To tell you I love you

Or to pray for your new adventure in this world

I Only

I only

Heard your sweet heartbeat

Felt your kicks when it was time to go to sleep

I only

Daydreamed about

What you would look like

Who you would be

How you might live your life

I only

Got to see your father overjoyed

By your movement

And the excitement family life

Had in store

I only
Wish I got the chance
To see it all come true

Alone in the Midst

The feeling of sadness
Controls her thoughts
Creating a need to feel his presence

She walks into his empty room
Filled with all his favorite things
Just how he left it that day
He never came home

She sits on his bed
Gazing at the picture on his nightstand
Of him and his best friend
Posing next to their cars

She grabs his pillow
Hugging it tight
Looking at all his favorite things

His first pair of football cleats
The MVP trophies
High School championship rings
The keyboard he played every Sunday before church

The tears gently roll down her cheeks
Breaking her heart
One memory at a time

She slowly lies down on his bed
Covering herself with his blue throw blanket
In hopes of feeling his embrace

Replaying "what if" and "if only"
In her head over and over again
Crying herself to sleep
In his bed

The Person I Once Was

When you were here

You were someone
Who made me smile

You were someone
Who made me happy

You were someone
Who loved spending time with me every day

You were someone
Who touched my body in a way no one else could

You were someone
Who stole my heart

As I am forced to move forward without you

I became someone
You wouldn't recognize
With no contagious smile or joy

I became someone
You would want to "snap out of it"
Releasing the guilt, I can't move forward from
Constantly wondering what I could have done to save you

I became someone
You would not be proud of
Losing sight of my focus
Letting go of the goals we set to accomplish

Sleep to Escape

Closing her eyes
She drifts off to sleep
In anticipation to see him again

Waking in her dreams
Walking down the beach in Hawaii
In a white summer dress
Enjoying the sand between her toes

There is a man in the distance
In his military uniform, walking towards her
Smiling as they lock eyes

Instantly, they begin running towards each other
He picks her up, spinning her around
As they intensely embrace each other

Their kiss is magical
Stopping time
Glistening with happiness in the sunlight

Once again,
They are together
In each other's arms

Their children come running up behind her
He holds everyone together as one
Overjoyed by the love they shared

The morning sun kissing her face too soon
Waking her to another day alone

But the happiness in her dreams
Is the escape she waits for every night

Love's Shackled Prisoner

Sitting home alone like a prisoner

Waiting for you to come back

To love me

The way you always did

The shackles of love weighing me down

Keeping me from moving forward

Staying loyal to the love I lost

A touch I crave only from you

One day

I will have the strength to break free

Removing the guilt of moving on

Releasing my soul tie

Accepting our life is over

Trusting I will survive

Allowing myself to be happy with another

Never replacing our love

But continuing my life

Until we are together again

Breathless Red Flannel Blanket

———❤———

Sitting down with her daughter and husband
One Saturday evening
In front of a warm, crackling fire
To enjoy a relaxing movie

All of a sudden
They hear this unforgettable sound
Someone was struggling upstairs
The feeling of fear struck their bodies

Instantly, the mother ran up the stairs
With her heart racing
Afraid of what she was going to find

She reached the bathroom door
With no response, she broke it open
To the horror
Of the red blanket wrapped around his neck
Holding him there lifeless

Stifling Invisible Voices

It's quiet
You no longer yell his name
Attempting to control his actions
Inflicting confusion and self-harm in his mind

It's peaceful
Knowing he can sleep
Trusting you will not scare him in the dark
Causing him endless sleepless nights

It's reassuring
Knowing he is free from the medication
That kept him one pill away
From hearing your voices again

It's comforting
Knowing one day
I will get to meet the part of my son
You stole from me

How to Be

Do I stay numb, ignoring my feelings
Or let people see me cry
To show them that I am human

Do I yell at everyone
Or let others make all the decisions
To avoid attempting to control the uncontrollable

Do I be myself
Or pretend to be ok
So I do not lose it

Do I smile to be grateful for the time we spent
Or praise God for taking you home safely
To not question His choice to take you from us

Falling Short

My self-care is not enough
To heal the wounds
Left behind

My desire to be ok is not enough
To exist in the world
Alone without you

My friend's support is not enough
To motivate me to reach my goals
My self-doubt destroys

Shattered Glass

The sledgehammer struck her heart
Fiercely with no warning
Shattering it like a glass vase
Into a million pieces

She lay on her bed, lifeless and in shock
Trying to recover from the loss

She regains her breath
Slowly starting to pick up the pieces

Some were large and easy to see
While others were invisible, cutting her skin

There were still a few slivers of her heart
She could never find

She searched for years
But those pieces of her heart were never the same
Still bleeding in silence

Until one day, she looked in the mirror
Realizing her lost pieces were the most important
But the hardest to see

Her reflection reminded her that
Acceptance, forgiveness, and love
Were the shattered pieces she had to heal
On her own from within

The Silent Daily Reminders

Two kids

One father

Together as a family

Without their mom

Guided by his pillar of strength

Even though he feels alone

With the light dimming around his heart

Losing hope from the storms life brings

Two children

One widowed father

To lead a broken home

Empowered by the accountability to stand alone

Even when he doesn't know how

The structure they instilled

Motivated him to continue leading his family to greatness

Two smiles

One love

A reflection of happiness

Dedicated to loving each other

Ensuring his children still understand the meaning of love

Sacrificing his needs

To continue the legacy they dreamed of

The Times We Shared

You blessed me before you met me

Naming me before you held me

Giving a gift from your heart

When I was little

We would take long car rides to see you

Walking to the beach twice a day

Just to see the ocean view

You took us to play bingo in the smoky halls

Made elegant wedding dresses

Crocheted me many afghans

And often laughed at silly cards in the store with my mom

As I grew

Becoming a single mother

You shared your single mother struggles with me

Showing me how strong and resourceful you were

Extending your kindness in the midst of my hardships
One time, lending me money you didn't have
Accepting a handwritten contract from me to re-pay you
Something no one ever did for me

You shared a part of your struggle with me
Many people never knew
Always allowing me to interrupt your Mariners' games
To warm my broken heart with your chocolate chip cookies

As you got older
Your memory was taken from you
One day at a time
Slowly stealing the grandma I held so close

I would come to see you
But eventually, you forgot who I was
Selfishly protecting myself from the pain
I stopped coming to see you
But I never stopped loving you

I would help my mom buy you Christmas gifts

Listen to my mom sadly drown in tears

In hope you would remember her for a moment

Many times, my mom asked me to say goodbye

Thinking it was your last day

But you were strong

Until I couldn't say goodbye again

And you finally let go

Holiday Spritz

Her daughter and grandchildren gather in the kitchen
Waiting to make their Great Grandma's Christmas spritz cookies

Each grandchild takes turns filling the spritz cookie tube
Putting the press on the end
And gently pushing the dough out into circles onto the cookie sheets

Overtime, the great cookie press got harder and harder to push
Her daughter tried to repair
But this year, it was falling apart

When the last cookie was made
The handle broke
Everyone sighed, and a little piece of their hearts broke
As they placed Great Grandma's cookie press in the box
Never to be used again

Every Sunday

She brings her chair
To sit in front of the fountain of memories
Visiting with the mother
She can no longer hold

She shares her stories
To keep her up to date on life's adventures
Including her in the world she is missing
Year after year

Reminiscing about their time together
Laughing about the memories
Reminding her how much she is still loved and missed
Day after day

She sheds tears
To release the pain
Trying to find the strength to move on without her
Minute by minute

She brings a planted flower
To reflect the color of her spirit
Proving something everlasting
One blooming bud at a time

Occasionally inviting her siblings
To visit their mother as one
As they did every week in the nursing home
Expressing the love in their hearts
Beat by beat

I Can't Wait

I can't wait
To feel my heart

No longer painfully bleeding
For the one taken from me

I can't wait
To heal the soul

No longer shattered into pieces
By the loss of the one that was the glue
That made me whole

I can't wait
To see the light
No longer blown out

Rekindling the passion

Rejoicing in faith

For the life we had the opportunity to share

The Melody of an Angel

As the music speaks to my broken heart
I'm at a loss for words

The sadness is clouding my vision
I pray you remove the smoke from my mind

Empower my thoughts into the path we shared
Giving me the direction I'm missing

Your memory and inspiration will always be alive
Continuously changing me

Even without
Your presence to guide me

The New Path

Closure

No celebration of life is the same
They all have a different name
Representing a different culture
Expressing a different way of life

Some are filled with laughter
Reminiscing about the good times
With food and music filling the air

Some are filled with a solid color
Representing a brotherhood, a family as one
With flags and symbols of the creed

Others are filled with heart-wrenching sorrow
Almost unbearable to all in attendance
With loved ones wailing in grief

Others culturally involve everyone
Respectfully filling the grave one shovel at a time
With a love for rich traditions

They may all look different on the outside
But on the inside
They all are honoring someone
Loved and lost

Nothing Else Matters

Today is the day
We come together
Putting all family feuds on pause
All feelings of disagreement aside
To remember the reason why we gather

We join together to celebrate the one we loved
The one we cherished
The one who deserves the honor

Through the ups and downs
We say goodbye
Until we see you again

Voice of Glory

The family slowly gathers around the graveside

All wearing purple or shirts with her face

They place her portraits on the easels

Arranging her flowers all around her casket

Setting up the speaker

The music starts

While a large group of family starts singing gospel

Joyfully, they harmonize, filling the air with love

The tribal leaders show their respects

Reciting verses in Samoan

Bringing their culture to life

As one

The family rejoices

Laughing at memories

Sharing the blessing in their hearts

Salute

The young grandchildren
Playfully walk down the cemetery rows
Looking at all the loved ones' markers

Some of them were removing vases
Setting them upright
In hope families would place flowers

Others were sitting on the benches
Waiting to say goodbye

As the cemetery grounds crew arrive
Removing the tent and chairs
Using the backhoe to carefully place the vault lid

The kids lay in a row side by side on the grass

As the truck slowly gets into place

They all stand at attention

Saluting their grandfather

As the dump truck shakes the dirt down onto the vault

Dust particles flowing in the air

As their faces shine with pride

Honoring the soldier they called Papa

This Is It

The cars park one by one
As family and friends slowly walk to the graveside
They embrace each other
Crying as the pallbearers carry their mother to rest

The pastor says a prayer
Allowing family to share story after story
Reminding each other of the good times
Spreading joy and laughter through the air

One by one, they all take a rose
Laying the flower softly on top of the casket
Next to the pallbearer's white gloves
Touching it one last time

The tears roll down everyone's cheeks
Watching the casket lower
Saying goodbye to the one they so dearly loved

Hugs Speak Volumes

Our family, friends, and new faces
Extending their arms bringing warmth
Safely surrounding us with love
Holding us up from crumbling to the ground

The power of a warm embrace
Speaks to our souls
Holding us close

Reminding us that people do care
Wanting to help
Supporting the new, unexpected journey
We are all forced to explore

Untouchables

We see

Our loved ones heartbroken

Stuck in a place of sadness

We hear

The needs of others

Reaching out for a solution to fill the emptiness

We touch

The hands of all the attendees

Paying their respects

We feel

Being strong for others

Gives them the strength to know they will be ok

We think

If we don't admit the pain

It will go away

The Group

—♥—

Today is the day
She pulls the folded-up flyer from her purse
Slowly opening it
Checking what time it starts

She put on her shoes very slowly
Knowing she is ready to take the next step
Saying goodbye to the children and the babysitter
She gets in the car

Hesitantly starting her vehicle
Clenching the steering wheel
With her head down
As the tears stream down her cheeks

She wipes her face

Looks in the rearview mirror

Checking how she looks

Reminding herself to just drive

She heads towards her destination

Breathing nervously

Encouraging herself that she will be ok

As she pulls into the parking lot at the funeral home

Her heart beats quickly

Filling her with anxiety

She gets out

Walks inside

Asking where the "Grieving with Others" group session is

There are about 10 people in a small area

She notices someone in the group

They embrace her

Welcoming her with open arms

Right then

She knew she was there for a reason

Blessed she finally had the courage to go

Ones to Remember

———— ♥ ————

The connections exchange when they share their stories
Healing their hearts one conversation at a time
With an understanding and realization
They are all going through this together

Their stories may be different
But their feelings of loss and navigating grief
Are something they all experience

These people who touch their souls in this process
Are people they never forget

New Anniversary

A year has passed
Since you were taken from me

Rejoicing in your legacy
Family and friends gather
Where you rest

To feast on your favorite foods
To sing your songs
To laugh about the old times we shared
To celebrate the joy you brought into our lives

Honoring the life you lived
The love you shared

Your legacy we celebrate
Keeping you alive in our hearts forever

The Eternal Flame

From the day we met
I know your presence was magical
You shined a light on my heart
Brighter than the sun

Warming my soul
From the inside-out
Beaming uncontrollable rays of laughter
Throughout my body

Molding our perspectives
Into one interchangeable flame
Burning fiercely in the night
Keeping us connected
No matter the distance

Forever Tied

The bonds that tie them together
Stay tightly intertwined

Minute by minute
Day by day

Each memory brings them closer
In spirit

Week after week
Month by month

Patiently waiting with a hole in their hearts
Anticipating their reunion

Year after year

Fire and Ice

You were the flame to my fire

With just a spark

You always ignited a love that swarmed through my body

A feeling no one can replace

You were the ice cube in my water

With just a drop

You quenched my thirst

Cooling my emotions

A calmness I yearn to feel

You were the star in the night

With just a glow

You guide my way

Keeping on the right path

A lead I miss following

Crisp Reality

As he steps out the door
The cold air takes his breath away
Creating a sudden hesitation to turn around

He closes his eyes
Pulling his scarf up over his face
Zipping up his jacket
Quickly putting on his gloves

He takes a deep breath
Reminding himself this is the new norm
Asking God for the strength to push through
Pushing through the challenge the weather may bring

Locking the front door
He turns around
Quickly walking towards his car
To face the cold world ahead

Solo

I stand here

In silence

Encouraging myself

Putting one foot in front of the other

Learning how to only see my footsteps

When I turn around

Creating a path

Guiding me on a new journey

Forcing me to walk alone

One day at a time

Unexpected Sorrow

Sitting at the coffee shop
Crafting an email for work

He hears an older lady
Laughing in the distance

She sounded just like his mother
Who passed a year ago

A smile came to his face
Along with a fond memory
Of his mother and his laughing together
In that same coffee shop

Instantly, his heart was overwhelmed
With a rush of sorrow, he could not shake

The tears slowly trickled down his face
He started to wipe them one by one
Taking a few deep breaths

Suddenly
The tears began streaming faster and faster
He started sniffing
Trying not to make a scene

As he quickly packed up his laptop
Putting everything into his black leather briefcase

He rushed out to his car
Leaning his head back in his seat

After crying for a few minutes
He calmly called his boss
Taking the rest of the day off

Laughing Alone

The laughter they shared was endless
Always brightening the darkest of days
Making their connection irreplaceable

Knowing their laughter is now an unforgettable memory
She has to accept the sound of only her laughter
Enjoying the jokes and humor to live on
Even if she is laughing alone

The Melody of Memories

The music
Brought a smile to her face

Reminding her
Of the love they made

Even though
Their time is over

The memories of them
Last forever

Until Next Time

Their connection was magical
Capturing their hearts every time

Their eyes read each other's souls
Never missing a moment

Their bodies moved in perfect harmony
Making a song only they heard

A never-ending connection
Entangling them forever

They may part ways
But he never completely said goodbye
To the passion in his heart

He just silently spent months and years
Missing the love they shared

Trying to fill a void
Only she could fill for him
And he could fill for her

So, he patiently waits
Until it is his turn to fly
And they meet again

Never the Same

Holidays

Birthdays

Vacations

Times that are never the same

Smiles

Laughter

Warmth

Something your presence always brought

Children

Family

Friends

All reminisce in efforts to keep our memories alive

In an Instant

One day
Just like that
They see each other

The passion will burn deep
The rare experience of what true love felt like
Will overjoy their hearts

Reminding them of the love they missed
As they hug
Never having to let each other go again

From Above

They soar together
Through the heavens

Holding hands
Basking in the glory before them

Finally joining as one
After years of separation

Occasionally, they look down on their legacy
Watching their family tree blossom
One new family member at a time

Seeing the elders
Pass down family traditions

Embracing their culture

One recipe and ceremony at a time

Warming their hearts

As they proudly watch their family build

From above

103

Through the Clouds

One cloudy day
She adventured on a quiet drive
Trying to find some peace
As she was missing her loving parents

Wishing she would see a sign of them along the way
The clouds overhead were thick
Showing no sign of parting

Suddenly, two beautiful sun rays beamed through the clouds
Bringing a smile to her face
Warming her heart

After Thoughts

Aftermath

In the beginning
People stop by
Bring warm, home-cooked meals
Emotionally check in on the family

But after the storm calms
They all go back to their regular lives
Healing their temporary sadness
Occasionally reminiscing about the good times
Laughing and embracing the love

The real time sets in
Trying to get out of bed
Functioning productively at work
Attempting to cope with the agony of the loss
While masking that you are ok

In the end

The only one that can reduce the pain

Is you taking the steps to heal

Wounds of the Heart

The wounds of the heart are many

Some become bruises

Healing over time

Remembered only when reminded of the moment

Some wounds heal with care

Leaving a scar

Reminding us of the pain we once endured for a season

Then there are those wounds that never stop bleeding

No matter how we try to heal them

Remembering that moment bleeds like the day it happened

We may cry about the love we miss

Seek guidance for healing

Even laugh about the good times with tears in our eyes

But those scars will bleed a little

Every time our hearts remember

Milestones

The steps to healing
Look different for us all

Some are slow and steading
Progressing naturally
Allowing one to heal
Learning to celebrate the life lost
Freeing them of pain

Others stop in motion
Stuck in a reoccurring devastation
Day in and day out
Not allowing them to move forward
Holding them hostage to the loss

Our steps can lead us to healing

As long as we move forward

Utilizing the tools to help us heal

One step at a time

Lessons of Loss

Love yourself enough
To ask for help

Love yourself enough
To heal the bleeding wounds

Love yourself enough
To get back to the person you once were

Love yourself enough
To not remain a victim

Love yourself enough
To be an advocate of strength to others
Sharing your path to surviving a loss

The True Reflection of Closure

As you get older
The desire for closure and healing
Never gets easier
They just look different

Instead of quickly filling with rage
Seeking closure from hurting others
We learn to take a moment of silence
To calm our spirit, we took time to heal

Instead of breaking down in tears
Yearning for closure in anyone's arms
We learn to talk to the right people
To heal our hearts from the inside out

Instead of isolation
Thinking closure comes from space
We learn to enjoy positive environments
To remind our souls that love doesn't only come from within

Freedom in Forgiveness

— ♥ —

Forgive others for the hurt
To free our minds from the trauma

Forgive others for the pain
They inflicted by taking someone you loved
To release the strongholds they have

Forgive others for the misunderstandings during a death
Ignited by the dysfunction in families
To free yourself from grudges created by money

Gifting you the strength to overcome
The trauma that comes with a passing

Be True

The only person
In the way of your healing is you
So, step aside

Quiet doubting yourself
Ignore your fears of being alone

Take time to reflect on your fears
Why you are staying numb, stifling the process

Understand why you sacrifice your recovery
Pretending you are ok
Knowing you're one step away from a breakdown

Learn how to move forward, celebrating the life lived
To free yourself from the past you wish was the present

About the Author

I grew up in Washington, where my entire family resided, for most of my life. So, we attended several funerals for family and friends at a young age. As a result, I experienced the process of sudden passings and death due to long-term illness, as well as the effects they have on everyone involved.

Some of these losses throughout my life were heartbreaking and brought instant tears to her eyes at the thought of it possibly taking many years for me to recover. In contrast, others who passed were more of a relief that the loved one was no longer suffering. This healing and grieving process allowed me to accept the passing of that loved one over time, so when it happened, it hurt a little less.

No matter how someone passed, the feelings and path to healing were all the same. I had to learn ways to cope with the loss, heal from the pain, and understand how to live on without them.

When we are on this path to healing, we often feel alone and that no one understands. We may act out, isolate ourselves, and not have the tools or understand how to move forward. This book reminds you that you are not alone and gives you the courage to survive your loss.

Thank You

Thank you for spending your time in my thoughts.
I would love to hear from you.

Connect with me on social media.
Instagram@Thoughtsoflisarenee

LinkedIn, Facebook, and TikTok at:
Author Lisa Renee Hutchins

YouTube at:
Thoughts of Lisa Renee Hutchins – Author

Email me your thoughts at Gmail.
thoughtsoflisarenee@gmail.com

www.authorlisareneehutchins.com

Stay amazing, and don't let your past define you!
It is only a lesson learned on your journey to greatness!

www.ingramcontent.com/pod-product-compliance
Lightning Source LLC
Chambersburg PA
CBHW060541100426
42742CB00013B/2413